Homework Help English

Ages 8–9
Key Stage 2/Year 4

Alan Gardiner

We're the Homework Helpers!

We've thought up lots of fun activities for you!

So grab your pens and pencils...

...and let's get started!

Longman
An imprint of **Pearson Education**

Harlow, England · London · New York · Reading, Massachusetts · San Francisco
Toronto · Don Mills, Ontario · Sydney · Tokyo · Singapore · Hong Kong · Seoul
Taipei · Cape Town · Madrid · Mexico City · Amsterdam · Munich · Paris · Milan

Series editors:
Stuart Wall & Geoff Black
With thanks to Val Mitchell for additional material and
Heather Ancient for editorial development work

These people helped us write the book!

A complete range of **Homework Helpers** is available.

		ENGLISH	MATHS	SCIENCE
Key Stage 1	Ages 5–6 Year 1	✓	✓	Science is not included in the National Tests at Key Stage 1
	Ages 6–7 Year 2	✓	✓	
Key Stage 2	Ages 7–8 Year 3	✓	✓	✓
	Ages 8–9 Year 4	✓	✓	✓
	Ages 9–10 Year 5	✓	✓	✓
	Ages 10–11 Year 6	✓	✓	✓

This tells you about all our other books.

Which ones have you got?

Pearson Education Limited
Edinburgh Gate, Harlow
Essex CM20 2JE, England
and Associated Companies throughout the world

© Pearson Education Limited 2000

The right of Alan Gardiner to be identified as author of this work has been asserted in accordance with the Copyright, Designs and Patents Act 1988

Extracts on pages 10, 20 and 54 are taken from *The Ladybird Dictionary* and *The Ladybird Thesaurus*, reproduced courtesy of Ladybird Books Ltd and Pearson Education (*page 10*: adapted introduction from *The Ladybird Thesaurus* (Ladybird, 1997) © Ladybird Books Ltd, 1997; *page 20*: adapted introduction from *The Ladybird Dictionary* (Ladybird, 1996) © Ladybird Books Ltd, 1996; *other text*: © Addison Wesley Longman, 1996 and 1997).

All rights reserved; no part of this publication may be reproduced, stored in any retrieval system, or transmitted in any form or by any means, electronic, mechanical, photocopying, recording, or otherwise without either the prior written permission of the Publishers or a licence permitting restricted copying in the United Kingdom issued by the Copyright Licensing Agency Ltd, 90 Tottenham Court Road, London W1P 0LP.

First published 2000

British Library Cataloguing in Publication Data
A catalogue entry for this title is available from the British Library

ISBN 0-582-38145-2

Printed in Great Britain by Henry Ling Ltd, at the Dorset Press, Dorchester, Dorset

This is for grown-ups!

Guidance and advice

Schools are now asked to set regular homework, even for young children. Government guidelines for Year 4 (ages 8–9) suggest $1\frac{1}{2}$ hours of homework a week. Children are also encouraged to do at least 10–20 minutes of reading each day.

The Literacy Hour

The daily Literacy Hour was introduced into schools in September 1999. During this session, teachers focus on three broad areas: word, sentence and text. The aim of the Literacy Hour is to develop a child's reading and writing skills.

All the activities in this book are written to complement the Literacy Hour. The emphasis is on short, enjoyable exercises designed to stimulate a child's interest in language. Each activity will take 10–20 minutes, depending on the topic, and the amount of writing and drawing.

Themes and topics

Throughout the book key words have been set in **bold** text – these highlight the themes and content of the activities, and provide a guide to the topics covered.

Encourage your child

Leave your child to do the activity on their own, but be available to answer any questions. Try using phrases like: That's a good idea! How do you think you could do it? What happens if you do it this way? These will encourage your child to think about how they could answer the question for themselves.

If your child is struggling …

Younger children might need help understanding the question before they try to work out an answer, and children who need help with reading or writing may need you to work with them. If your child is struggling with the writing, ask them to find the answer and then write it in for them. Remember even if your child gets stuck, be sure to tell them they are doing well.

The activities start on the next page! Have you got your pens and pencils ready?

Check the answers together

When they have done all they can, sit down with them and go through the answers together. Check they have not misunderstood any important part of the activity. If they have, try to show them why they are going wrong. Ask them to explain what they have done, right or wrong, so that you can understand how they are thinking.

You will find answers to the activities at the back of this book. You can remove the last page if you think your child might look at the answers before trying an activity. Sometimes there is no set answer because your child has been asked for their own ideas. Check that your child's answer is appropriate and shows they have understood the question.

Be positive!

If you think your child needs more help with a particular topic try to think of some similar but easier examples. You don't have to stick to the questions in the book – ask your own: Did you like that? Can you think of any more examples? Have a conversation about the activity. Be positive, giving praise for making an effort and understanding the question, not just getting the right answers. Your child should enjoy doing the activities and at the same time discover that learning is fun.

More on Spelling

Help your child to keep a list of words that they tend to spell incorrectly. Encourage your child to use these words regularly in their own writing, so as to get into the habit of spelling them correctly. Help your child break down words into separate sounds or syllables ('home-work', 'read-ing'). This makes the spelling and reading of unfamiliar words easier.

Children can test themselves in the following way:
- **Look** at the word
- **Say** the spelling out loud
- **Cover** the word so they can't see it
- **Write** it down
- **Check** that it's spelt correctly

Poems, songs and nursery rhymes can help with a child's spellings because they encourage children to develop an awareness of sound patterns and an understanding of the link between sounds and letters.

Feeding time!

Charlie the chimp has mixed up all the fruit meant for the zoo animals. You can help sort out the mess by arranging the fruits in **alphabetical order**.

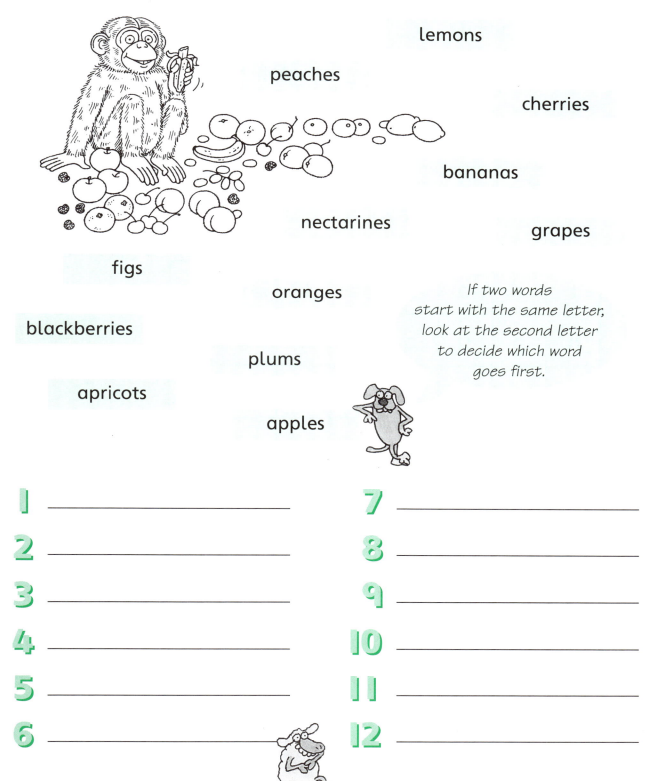

lemons

peaches

cherries

bananas

nectarines

grapes

figs

oranges

blackberries

If two words start with the same letter, look at the second letter to decide which word goes first.

plums

apricots

apples

1 _____   7 _____

2 _____   8 _____

3 _____   9 _____

4 _____   10 _____

5 _____   11 _____

6 _____   12 _____

Word hunt

These words all have the letters ou in them:

found   round   pound

ought   thought   brought

In this list, the letters ou make one sound when they are followed by nd and a different sound when they are followed by ght. Try to find these six words in the wordsearch below.

You need to look across, down and diagonally.

t	r	o	n	i	k	n	q
h	p	u	d	b	s	g	h
o	x	r	f	r	p	s	r
u	l	m	c	o	o	u	o
g	w	a	g	u	u	z	u
h	v	x	h	g	n	n	n
t	p	o	n	h	d	h	d
o	u	g	h	t	e	i	t

Can you think of any other words with ou in them? What sound does ou make in these?

Similar words

Sort these words into pairs with **similar meanings**. One pair has been done for you.

*Words with similar meanings are called **synonyms**.*

protect
procession   brave
            mail
    occasionally
final
            rare
    seashore
post   apartment
        guard   beach
unusual   parade
heroic sometimes   drizzle
                flat
        last
        shower

final, last   _____

_____   _____

_____   _____

_____   _____

Past or present?

Can you sort out this jumble of verbs by colouring the **past tense** and **present tense** of each verb the same colour.

The past tense tells us about something that has already happened.

catch

knew

speak

lead

stood

spoke

broke

go

saw

know

went

caught

keep

see

thought

stand

kept

led

think

break

The present tense is used when something is happening now.

Find the nouns

Draw a circle round each of the **nouns** in this list. You should be able to find ten altogether. Decide whether they are **common**, **proper** or **collective** nouns and write them in the correct column at the bottom of the page.

Collective nouns name groups of things.

Proper nouns name people, places or particular things. They start with a capital letter.

neat

thirsty

team

brilliant

ship

stormy

difficult

pale

tribe

Apollo

delicious

swarm

courage

Russia

sharp

steep

flowers

strong

Suzanne

cinema

Common nouns are the ordinary naming words.

Common nouns	Proper nouns	Collective nouns
_____	_____	_____
_____	_____	_____
_____	_____	_____
_____	_____	_____
_____	_____	_____

In other words...

Here are three extracts from a **thesaurus**. The first extract introduces the thesaurus and explains how it is set out. The other extracts show you what you would find if you looked up the words eat and enter.

About your Thesaurus

There are 2000 entries in this thesaurus, listed in alphabetical order, and finding the word or phrase you want is very easy.

Suppose you've used the word 'important' twice and you don't want to use it again. If you look up **important**, you'll see this:

numbers and examples show the different meanings of the word you looked up

example of the word you looked up

important 1 *(an important letter)* the **main** roads, the **principal** reasons, the **essential** ingredients, **key** facts, an **urgent** phone call, **necessary** information 2 *(an important person)* a **leading** scientist, a **first-class** artist, a **famous** singer, a **well-known** writer, a **great** building, a **top** athlete, a **world-class** tennis player

*words in **dark** letters show you other words for **important***

phrases show you how the word is used

eat *(eating chocolate)* They **devoured** the cake. The kids **consumed** all the crisps. Here's a sandwich to **chew**. She **nibbled** a biscuit. I can't **swallow** this meat. You **scoffed** the lot! Don't **bolt** your food. He **munched** an apple. Here's your tea, **tuck in**! Cows and sheep **feed** on grass. Budgies **live on** seeds.

enter 1 *(entering the classroom)* **Come in**, children. **Go in** and take off your wet clothes. The thieves **broke in** through the window. 2 *(entering a contest)* Mark wants to **join in** the race. Why don't you **put your name down for** the club? You can **enrol in** our next class. Anyone can **take part in** our carnival. 3 *(Enter your name on the screen.)* **Input** your data now. **Type in** the password first.

Now answer these questions!

1. How many words or phrases does the thesaurus give for eat? (Remember, other words or phrases are in dark letters.) _____

2. How many different meanings does the thesaurus give for enter? (Remember each different meaning is numbered.) _____

3. Can you explain the difference between nibbled and devoured?
   _____
   _____

4. Copy out the following sentence, changing the word enter to a different word or phrase.

   Susan decided to enter the egg and spoon race.
   _____
   _____

5. Here are three more words beginning with e. For each word, list as many words or phrases with a similar meaning as you can.

   excellent _____
   _____

   exclaimed _____
   _____

   expand _____
   _____

Food crossword

Here's a crossword where all the answers have something to do with food!

12

ACROSS

1 A baker makes this. (5 letters)

4 You might have this with milk for breakfast. (6 letters)

6 If you grill the answer to 1 Across until it's brown you get this. (5 letters)

7 A hot drink. (6 letters)

DOWN

1 You might have one or two of these with a cup of 2 Down. (8 letters)

2 This hot drink is made from leaves. (3 letters)

3 Apples and bananas are examples of this kind of food. (5 letters)

5 This is green and is usually part of a salad. (7 letters)

Adjective extra

These two pages are all about adjectives.

First find the adjectives in the jumble of words below. Then write them in the spaces at the bottom of the page.

Remember: adjectives are words that describe nouns.

cook   pull

glorious
      sad
   paint   disappointing

artist   boil   sky
                      tornado

wonderful   essential   dangerous
                                    round

              moist   clean
shelf
         path   stick

There are ten adjectives to find altogether.

        tough

_____   _____

_____   _____

_____   _____

_____   _____

In the spaces, write three adjectives that might be used with each of these nouns. One set of adjectives has been done for you.

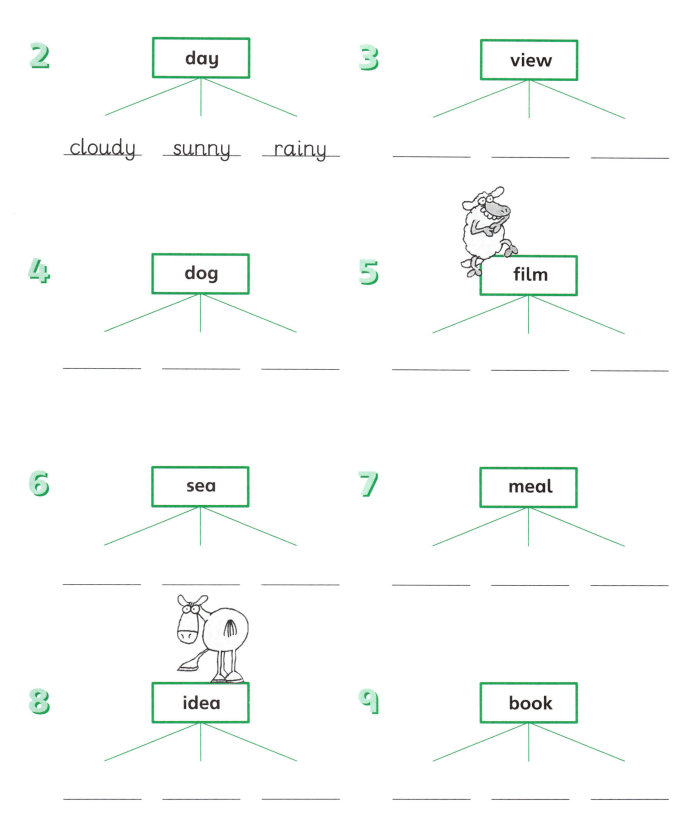

2 day — cloudy sunny rainy

3 view

4 dog

5 film

6 sea

7 meal

8 idea

9 book

Molly's birthday

This piece of writing has ten **spelling mistakes**. They have all been underlined. Write the correct spellings in the spaces underneath the story.

My big bruther John is good at art. He somtimes helps me to make things. My friend Molly loves swiming and when it was her burthday I asked John if he would help me make a diffrent type of card for Molly. We set to work. John showed me how to fold and cut the stiff papper and soon I had made a lovely pop-up card of Molly splashing in the water.

Later that day Molly was having a special pool party. The pool had lots of baloons in it. It looked grate. All the chilldren changed their cloathes and put on their costumes. It was a really good party, and Molly loved the card I had made!

_____ _____

_____ _____

_____ _____

_____ _____

_____ _____

Opposites

Sort these words into pairs of **opposites**. One pair has been done for you.

*Words that have opposite meanings are called **antonyms**.*

distant

dry   true   untidy

never   smooth   dull

bright

neat   quiet

wet   noisy   hairy

false   uneven   near

bald

certain   always

unsure

Can you think of some more pairs of opposites?

wet, dry

Word hunt

1 These words all have a **double consonant** in the middle:

> bubble   settle   kettle
> meddle   common   hammer

Try to learn these spellings if you don't know them already.

Remember: a,e,i,o and u are vowels. All the other letters are consonants.

Can you find these words in the wordsearch below? You need to look across, down and diagonally.

l	s	c	o	m	m	o	n
b	a	h	k	m	v	a	o
u	s	a	e	l	l	e	h
b	x	e	t	g	m	d	a
b	w	e	t	f	s	d	m
l	r	s	l	t	r	n	m
e	e	d	e	a	l	p	e
s	m	e	d	d	l	e	r

Try making your own wordsearch using the words you have written here.

2 What other words do you know with double consonants in the middle? Write some of them here.

_____

_____

Storytime

*This is a **writing frame** for a story.*

Stories need a **beginning**, a **middle** and an **end**.

The beginning and the end are here. Make up the middle of the story. Use the questions to help you.

> Suddenly the room began to fill with blue mist and the bed started to change into a small rowing boat. Peter held on to his pillow and wondered what would happen next.

What was Peter like?   What happened next?

Where did he go in the boat?   What happened first?

What did the place he went to look like?   Who did he meet?

_____

_____

_____

_____

_____

_____

_____

> The mist cleared and the familiar bedroom came into view. The boat became a safe, comfortable bed. Peter was home.

Dictionary quiz

Here are two extracts from a **dictionary**. The first extract introduces the dictionary and explains how it works. The second extract shows some words and their meanings or **definitions**. Read the information on this page, then answer the questions on the opposite page.

About your Dictionary

This easy to use dictionary contains 4000 words and abbreviations, listed in alphabetical order.

Your dictionary will help you to check and learn how to spell words, and to find out what each word means.

Each entry gives the way the word is used in a sentence, and which part of speech it is, eg noun, verb, etc.

The small figures at the beginning of the words as in ¹**saw**, ²**saw**, ³**saw**, show that each similar word has a separate use or meaning, and the most usual is given first. When a word has two main meanings that are the same part of speech, again the most usual appears first.

---

crocodile *noun* a large reptile that lives on land and in lakes and rivers in the hot wet parts of the world

crooked *adjective* not straight; bent; **crookedly** *adverb*; **crookedness** *noun*

crop *noun* **1** a plant or part of a plant such as grain, fruit, or vegetables grown by a farmer; **2** the amount of grain, vegetables, etc, cut and gathered at one time

¹**cross** *noun* **1** a figure or mark formed by one straight line crossing another; anything shaped like x or +; **2** an animal or plant that is a mixture of breeds

²**cross** *verb* **1** to go, pass, or reach over or across; **2** to cause an animal or plant to breed with one of another kind; **crossing** *noun*

³**cross** *adjective* angry; bad-tempered; **crossly** *adverb*

crow *noun* a large shiny black bird with a loud rough cry

crowd *noun* a large number of people gathered together; **crowded** *adjective*

1. How many different meanings are given for the word crop?
   _____

2. What meaning does cross have when it is used as an adjective?
   _____

3. What adjective is formed from the noun crowd?
   _____

4. Which two words in this dictionary would you put crouch between?
   _____
   _____

   Remember the words in a dictionary are listed in alphabetical order.

   Do you know what crouch means? If not, try looking it up in a dictionary!

5. Here are some more words beginning with the letter c. How would you explain their meaning? Are they nouns, verbs or adjectives? Write in your answers. Compare them with the definitions in a real dictionary if you can.

   cucumber

   _____
   _____

   customer

   _____
   _____

21

Describe it

The man drove a car down the lane.
This does not tell you very much about the man or the car.
Adjectives make writing more interesting.

The *elderly* man drove an *old-fashioned* car down the *winding* lane.

An adjective describes a noun.

Adverbs help describe how he drove.

The elderly man drove an old-fashioned car *slowly* down the winding lane.

An adverb describes a verb.

Make this sentence more interesting.

The lady drove her car along the motorway.

_____

Choose characters and cars from the illustration to make your own sentences.

_____

_____

_____

22

To, too and two

Read this story and every time there is a gap, write in one of the following: **to**, **too** or **two**.

Too can mean **as well**, and is also used in phrases like **too much**.

Dad was taking me and some friends (1) _____ the newsagents. We each had (2) _____ pounds (3) _____ spend.

'Don't forget Sammy,' Mum said.

'Does he have (4) _____ come?' I complained.

'Yes,' said Dad, 'Sammy comes (5) _____ .'

When we got (6) _____ the shop, it took us some time (7) _____ decide what (8) _____ buy. Some things were much (9) _____ expensive. At last we all picked what we wanted (10) _____ buy, and we all had change from our (11) _____ pounds.

We bought Sammy a little toy car with the change. Sammy's nearly (12) _____ and he thought the car was great. I've never seen him so happy! I was glad Sammy came with us after all.

Write some sentences of your own using **to**, **too** and **two**.

_____

_____

23

Find the verbs

1 Find the **verbs** in this jumble of words. Write them in the spaces at the bottom of the page.

Remember: verbs are doing words.

There are ten verbs to find altogether.

wade   chimney   write   think   magical   meet   greet   squash   add   gardener   leader   river   acrobat   break   exclaim   nearly   hair   heavy   surfer   carry

_____   _____

_____   _____

_____   _____

_____   _____

_____   _____

2 Can you write four sentences of your own, each using a different one of these verbs?

_____

_____

_____

_____

Sounds the same

1 Look at the words on this page and sort them into eight pairs of words that **rhyme**. One has been done for you.

Be careful – words with the same letters don't always make the same sounds!

could
bone
tough
hour   stone
four
dough
none   sour
pour
would
bough
rough
done
though   plough

hour, sour _____   _____

_____   _____

_____   _____

2 Can you use some of these words to make a nonsense rhyme?

_____

_____

_____

_____

Calendar chaos

On this page you'll find the twelve months of the year, but not one of them has been spelt correctly! Write the **correct spelling** for each month in the space provided.

Get someone to check your spellings before you try to put the words in order.

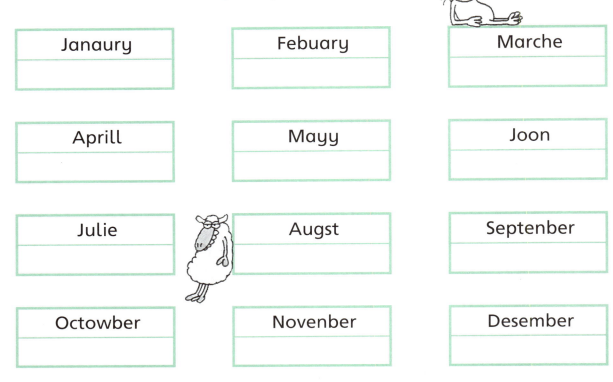

Janaury	Febuary	Marche
April	Mayy	Joon
Julie	Augst	Septenber
Octowber	Novenber	Desember

Now write the months out again, arranging them in **alphabetical order**.

1 _____
2 _____
3 _____
4 _____
5 _____
6 _____
7 _____
8 _____
9 _____
10 _____
11 _____
12 _____

26

Changing words

Turn the top word into the bottom one by changing one letter at a time. The first one has been done for you.

1. bend
   bent
   beat
   boat
   goat

2. fall
   _____
   _____
   _____
   pest

3. moon
   _____
   _____
   _____
   beat

4. race
   _____
   _____
   _____
   fist

5. past
   _____
   _____
   _____
   sore

6. fare
   _____
   _____
   _____
   mint

Now try making up some for yourself.

What's the difference?

There	In that place	The paper shop is over there.
Their	Belonging to them	Their team won the hockey match.
They're	short for they are	They're coming with us.

Write there, their or they're in each space.

1 _____ was a special match on down at the recreation ground.

2 The two teams were wearing _____ away strip.

3 "_____ aren't very many people here," said Peter.

4 "_____ all on holiday this week," replied Dad.

5 "_____ socks are different this week," commented Uncle Dave. "But don't worry, _____ will be some on sale in the club shop."

6 _____ were lots of fans with _____ children at the shop.

Hunt the adverb

1 Circle the **adverbs** in the passage below. There are six altogether. One has already been found, so you need to find another five.

'Put it down, Megan!' I shouted (loudly) at my little sister.

'Shush, Peter, you'll frighten him,' she whispered quietly.

'How can you frighten a slippery, slimy snail?' I laughed.

Megan looked hurt and I felt a bit guilty. 'He can have some of my sandwich,' I said, placing a lettuce leaf on the lawn.

Megan carefully placed the snail on the leaf. It quickly and very greedily munched away. Megan smiled happily.

Adverbs usually end in ly.

Adverbs describe actions.

Now think of an adverb to complete each of these sentences:

2 I was in a hurry so walked very _____ to school.

3 She tickled me _____ on the nose with a feather.

4 Harry spoke quite _____ to the old man.

5 I held the glass bowl very _____ .

Where do I find it?

This is the **contents page** of a book about Ancient Egypt. After you have looked at it, answer the questions on the opposite page.

THE AGE OF THE EGYPTIANS

Contents

Chapter 1	Who were the Egyptians?	5
Chapter 2	Cities of Ancient Egypt	15
Chapter 3	The Pyramids and the Royal Tombs	27
Chapter 4	The Sphinx	37
Chapter 5	The River Nile	41
Chapter 6	Kings and Queens of Egypt	49
	Tutankhamun	55
	Cleopatra	59
Chapter 7	Everyday Life in Ancient Egypt	65
Chapter 8	Writing in Ancient Egypt	77
Chapter 9	Religion	81
Index		87

1. What is the number of the chapter that tells you how ordinary Egyptians lived? _____

2. If you wanted to find out about the rulers of Ancient Egypt, which page would you turn to? _____

3. Thebes was a city in Ancient Egypt. Which chapter might you look at to find information about it? _____

4. If you wanted to know about the gods that were worshipped by the Ancient Egyptians, which page would you turn to? _____

5. Tutankhamun was a king of Egypt. When he died he was buried with a great deal of treasure in a tomb in the Valley of the Kings. Which two chapters would you look at to find out about Tutankhamun's life and death? _____

6. Write three questions of your own about this contents page. Write down where you will find the answers to your questions.

_____

_____

_____

_____

_____

_____

Speech marks are also called inverted commas.

I say

Speech marks are used to show words that are actually spoken:

"My fire's gone out!" said the little dragon.

You need a comma before starting the speech marks if you are told who is speaking before them:

Speech marks show you where to change your tone for different characters' voices when you read aloud.

The knight said, "I will help you to light it again."

You need a comma before closing the speech marks if you are told who is speaking after them:

"I will help you to light it again," the knight said.

Watch out for question marks. These come before the speech marks.

"Do you really think that you can help?" asked the little dragon.

Rewrite these sentences. Put the speech marks in the correct places.

1 I'll find you some special fire weed replied the knight kindly.

_____

_____

2 The little dragon said Does it taste nice?

_____

3 It's a little peppery the knight remarked.

_____

If the sentence carries on after you're told who's speaking, you need a comma before the next set of speech marks.

4 I think said the little dragon I might like it. (Be careful – you need two sets of speech marks and two commas here!)

_____

5 Don't eat it so quickly shouted the knight You'll get hiccups!

_____

_____

6 I don't think that is going to work cried the little dragon.

_____

7 Try clearing your throat laughed the knight.

_____

8 Ahhhhhh! coughed the little dragon That's much better!

_____

9 Ow! yelled the knight I'm going home before you do any more damage.

_____

Commas

You don't need a comma after the last adjective!

Commas are needed to separate adjectives when there is more than one – a large, hairy dog; a smooth, purple fruit; a cold, muddy, boring walk.

Add commas to these sentences. Circle any letters that should be capitals, and add full stops too.

1. i wore tight yellow flowery leggings

2. it was the biggest shiniest spottiest ball i had ever seen

3. grandad had a tiny cluttered wooden shed

4. the kittens made small mewling pitiful cries

*Careful – if two adjectives are joined by **and** they don't need a comma!*

5. the vikings were said to be fierce bloodthirsty and merciless warriors

6. my friend was clever pretty and talented

7. Think of some sentences of your own using adjectives and commas.

_____
_____
_____
_____
_____
_____

Commas are also needed in lists of nouns.

> I needed a saw, wood, glue and screws to make the table.

Put the commas in these lists.

*Don't forget, if two nouns in a list are joined by **and** they don't need a comma.*

8 Mum had bread tea bacon eggs and milk on her shopping list.

9 I saw soap shampoo conditioner bubble bath toothpaste and toothbrushes on our bathroom shelf.

10 There were Alsatians Dalmatians Labradors poodles and greyhounds at the dog show.

11 Miss Old Mr Dobbs Mr Chang Mrs Wart and my dad are going on the school trip.

12 We had snow rain hail and sunshine on Thursday morning.

13 Now make up some of your own lists of nouns and show where the commas should go.

_____

_____

_____

_____

_____

_____

Making adjectives

1. Match the words on the left with the **suffixes** on the right to form five adjectives. Write them in the spaces below.

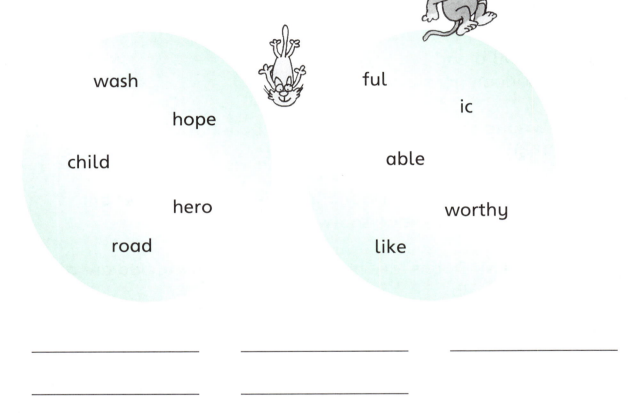

A suffix is a group of letters found at the end of a word.

wash   hope   child   hero   road

ful   ic   able   worthy   like

_____   _____   _____

_____   _____

2. Now make adjectives from the words below. Use the same suffixes as before. One has been done for you.

trust   <u>trustworthy</u>

care   _____

life   _____

angel   _____

read   _____

Can you make more adjectives by adding these suffixes to words that you know?

36

LS

Rhymes with ...

Sort the words shown on this page into eight pairs of words that **rhyme**.

This is pretty tricky. The words rhyme but they don't use the same letters!

phone
mane
grow
great   worm
        crate
                groan
rain
    crowd
            though   haze
    group
            loop   squirm
                days
            loud

One has been done for you.

crowd, loud

Secret code

At the bottom of the page is a message in **code**. If you study the letters in the top half of the page, you should be able to work out how the code works.
Write the missing letters in the boxes, then decode the message. Good luck!

a	b	c	d	e	f	g	h	i	j
z	y	x	w						

k	l	m	n	o	p	q	r	s	t

u	v	w	x	y	z

Decode means to work out what the message says.

x	l	m	t	i	z	g	f	o	z	g	r	l	m	h

b	l	f	e	v

x	i	z	x	p	v	w

g	s	v

x	l	w	v

!

Try inventing your own code!

Rivers and mountains

On the left are some words you might need if you were writing about the countryside or the sea. On the right are their meanings, but they are in the wrong order. Draw lines to join each word to the correct **definition**.

1. river

2. cliff

3. lake

4. mountain

5. coast

6. waterfall

- the land next to the sea
- a very high hill
- water falling straight down over rocks
- a wide, natural stream of water
- a high, steep piece of land close to the sea
- a large area of water, surrounded by land

Its or it's

| Its | means it belongs to someone or something: | The cat licked its paw. |
| It's | is short for it is: | It's a windy night. (*It is* a windy night.) |

Write these sentences out again using it is instead of it's.

1 It's dark tonight.

_____

2 It's launch day tomorrow.

_____

3 It's an exciting programme.

_____

Write its or it's in the spaces.

4 The spacecraft hovered in the sky, _____ lights flashing.

5 The spacecraft gained speed on _____ mission into space.

6 "_____ my first space flight," shouted Rebecca.

In front

Can you fill in the **meanings** of these words?

These **prefixes** are all to do with numbers.

1 bi means two

bicycle _____

binoculars _____

2 tri means three

tricycle _____

triangle _____

3 quad means four

quadrangle _____

quadruplets _____

4 pent means five

pentagon _____

pentathlon _____

5 cent means hundred

centimetre _____

century _____

Use a dictionary to find the meaning of any words you don't know.

Festival fun

Here is a poster for a cartoon festival. When you have read it, answer the questions on the opposite page.

CARTOON FESTIVAL
A weekend of fun for all the family!

An exhibition of classic cartoons in the Town Hall

Have your portrait drawn by a famous cartoonist in Hamilton Park

A special demonstration by prizewinning cartoonist Howard Riley (in the Town Hall 3 p.m. 25 July)

- Other events on both days in the Town Hall
- Many of Britain's most famous cartoonists will be in nearby Hamilton Park throughout the weekend
- The Mayor of Birkdale will open the event at 10 a.m. on 24 July
- Festival times: Saturday 24 July and Sunday 25 July 10 a.m. – 5 p.m.
- For more information ring 0157 793 8462

Ample car parking will be available, or get to the Festival by bus (18, 55, 63) or train (Birkdale Station)

1. Where will the exhibition of classic cartoons take place?

   _____

   You'll need to read the whole poster carefully.

2. On what dates will the festival take place?

   _____

3. Where will you be able to have your portrait drawn by a cartoonist?

   _____

4. Who is going to open the festival?

   _____

5. Which train station would you travel to for the festival?

   _____

6. What will be the date and time for the demonstration by Howard Riley?

   _____

7. The poster suggests three different ways to get to the festival – what are they?

   _____

8. What would you do if you wanted more information about the festival?

   _____

I'd like to be drawn by a cartoonist! Would you?

Take it away

*If you take away letters from the beginning of a word, you're taking away a **prefix**.*

Make new words by taking letters away from either the beginning or the end of these words. Two have been done for you.

*If you take away letters from the end of a word, you're taking away a **suffix**.*

1. mistake — take
2. gradually — gradual
3. triangle —
4. mislead —
5. astonishment —
6. afterwards —
7. talking —
8. hopeful —
9. bicycle —
10. really —
11. unusual —
12. return —

Can you make some new words with the prefixes you've taken away? e.g. misfortune

How was it done?

Adverbs tell you more about the verb.

| He gobbled hungrily. | He shouted angrily. | She cried silently. |

Use adverbs to make these sentences more interesting.

The monster roared _____

The goblin giggled _____

The elf disappeared _____

The boy jumped down and fell _____

Try starting sentences with adverbs. They can make your writing more exciting.

The first has been done for you.

Silently the mist rose from the hidden lake and swirled towards the boat house.

Suddenly _____

Desperately _____

Frantically _____

Eventually _____

Similes

| as light as a feather | as quiet as a mouse | as brave as a lion |

1 These are **similes**. We use them to describe a thing by comparing it with something else. Similes are well-known and often well-used phrases.

Can you finish these similes?

as fast as a _____   as wise as an _____

as cunning as a _____   as sweet as _____

as green as _____   as white as a _____

2 Complete these sentences with a simile.

The knight was trembling like a _____

The dragon's breath was as hot as _____

The king was as proud as a _____

The winter's earth was hard as _____

Using similes can make your writing more interesting.

3 Now choose your own word to finish these similes. Think of words that make a good description.

as cool as a _____   as _____ as a whistle

as happy as a _____   as _____ as snow

Sort them out!

The answers to these picture clues all start with the letter **f**. Write the correct word under each picture.

7 Now write the words out again, this time arranging them in **alphabetical order**.

Remember you may need to look at the second or third letters of the words to put them in order.

 # Double trouble

The answers to these clues are words that can mean more than one thing. The same word matches the clue on the left and the clue on the right. One has been done for you.

1. Used in cricket (bat) A creature that flies at night

2. A place that looks after your money (_____) The side of a river

3. Not heavy (_____) Opposite of dark

4. This tells you how much you have to pay (_____) A bird's beak

5. You use this to draw a straight line (_____) Someone in charge of a country

6. A place where you might play or walk your dog (_____) You do this when you stop in a car

7. Twelve inches (_____) This has five toes

8. You stick this on a letter (_____) You might do this with your foot if you're angry

Can you find some more words that have two different meanings?

Past and present

Fill in the gaps to complete the pairs of **present** tense and **past tense** verbs. One has been done for you.

Take care over your spelling in this exercise!

1. drink / drank
2. stop /
3. sleep /
4. slip /
5. ___ / kept
6. hurry /
7. ___ / worried
8. ___ / left
9. ___ / fell
10. am /

Sorting words

Here is a piece of writing about castles. Read it then answer the questions on the opposite page.

The earliest castles were built of wood, but later they were built of stone. With their high towers and thick walls they were very strong. They needed strong defences because they had to protect the people who lived inside the castle from attack. Many castles also had deep ditches all the way around them. These were called moats. Armies that were attacking the castle would try to climb the walls or force their way in with battering rams. Those inside would fire arrows at the enemy soldiers. Sometimes their attackers would surround the castle until the people inside ran out of food and had to surrender.

Can you find the following in the passage you have just read?

- Five **nouns**
- Five **verbs**
- Five **conjunctions**
- Five **adjectives**

Conjunctions are joining words that link parts of a sentence.

To help you get started, one of each has already been found for you.

1. Nouns

castles

2. Verbs

needed

3. Conjunctions

but

4. Adjectives

earliest

Making marks

Speech marks show that someone is saying something – they go before and after the words that are spoken.

"Here I am," she replied.

> **Question marks** show that a question is being asked – "Where are you?"
>
> **Exclamation marks** give emphasis to the sentence – "Stop it!"

Use an exclamation mark to show surprise, excitement, a command, a threat or anger.

Put in the right punctuation marks in these sentences:

1. Give it to me at once
2. I'm knitting a scarf, she explained
3. What's the score
4. How many do you want
5. I'm very sleepy, she replied
6. Put that back
7. Why do you want it
8. I enjoy watching videos, he said
9. Go away, she cried
10. Where am I

Don't forget you may need to use full stops.

Comparatives

By changing an adjective, you can compare two things –
My grandad is old, but my grandma is older.

Old is the adjective and older is the **comparative**.

To make the comparative, you normally add er to the adjective.

If the adjective ends in y, you must change the y into i and then add er.

Ring the comparatives in these sentences.

1. Your dog is small, but mine is smaller.

2. I am always hungrier than you.

3. My feet are smellier than yours.

4. The tunnel was dark, but the cave was darker.

5. My brother's voice is loud, but yours is louder.

If the adjective ends in e, you just add r.

Now think of some adjectives you can change into the comparative. Here are two to start you off:

_____large_____ / _____   _____windy_____ / _____

_____ / _____   _____ / _____

_____ / _____   _____ / _____

53

Dictionary Quiz

Here are some more words and **definitions** from a dictionary.

jar *noun* a container like a bottle with a short neck and wide mouth

javelin *noun* a light throwing spear used in sport

jaw *noun* either of the two face bones which hold the teeth

jazz *noun* a type of music with a strong beat

jealous *adjective* **1** wanting to get what somebody else has; **2** being afraid of losing what you have; **jealously** *adverb*; **jealousy** *noun*

jeans *noun* strong cotton trousers that are often blue

jelly *noun* a soft food that shakes when moved

jersey *noun* a sweater

jet *noun* **1** a type of aircraft that has a **jet engine**; **2** a narrow stream of liquid, gas, etc, forced through a small hole

Jew *noun* a person belonging to the worldwide group descended from the people of ancient Israel and practising their religion; **Jewish** *adjective*

jewel *noun* a precious stone, used as an ornament

jewellery or **jewelry** *noun* ornaments with jewels

jigsaw puzzle or **jigsaw** *noun* a picture made up of pieces which have to be fitted together

job *noun* **1** a piece of work; **2** regular work for which you are paid

jockey *noun* a person who rides in horse races

jog *verb* **(jogged) 1** to run slowly and steadily; to run like this to keep fit; **2** to shake or push slightly; **jog** *noun*; **jogger** *noun*; **jogging** *noun*

join *verb* **1** to fasten together; to connect; **2** to become a member of a group; **join** *noun*

54

1 What must an aeroplane have in order to be called a jet?
_____

2 Why does the word Jew begin with a capital letter? (Clue: Do you know what type of noun the word is – common, proper or collective?)
_____

3 What name is used to refer to a person who jogs?
_____

4 If you were to add the word jingle to the dictionary, where would it go?
_____

5 Here are three more words beginning with j. Write your own explanations of what the words mean, then compare your definitions with the ones in a dictionary.

Remember to say if these words are nouns or verbs.

January _____

_____

juggle _____

_____

junior _____

_____

Thank you letters

When you write a **thank you letter**, think about the person you are writing to. What will they be interested in?

The most important part is to say 'thank you' so that needs to be the first thing that you write.

Say what you bought if they sent you money, or whether you enjoyed using or playing with the present.

Remember! Letters are set out in a special way.

Your address is written here on the right hand side at the top followed by the date

Dear _____ ,

Indent your first line of writing on the line below.
End your letter at the bottom.
Don't forget to put who it's from.

Remember! There are lots of ways of finishing letters.

Letters starting 'Dear Sir' should finish 'Yours faithfully'

Letters starting 'Dear Mr/Mrs/Miss/Master Jones' should finish 'Yours sincerely'

Letters starting 'Dear Chris' should finish 'Your friend, love from'

Now try writing a thank you letter to your great-aunt for sending you an amusing present. It could be something really strange like a live hippopotamus or an alien.

Adverb extra

1. Pick out all the **adverbs** in the jumble of words below. You should be able to find ten. Write them in the spaces at the bottom of the page.

Remember: adverbs describe actions and they usually end in **ly**.

noisy
sly
powerfully
curly
hurriedly
immediate
fly
gradually
craftily
nasty
tenderly
final
carefully
loudly
quick
tidy
energetically
affectionately
tiny
cleverly
necessary
smelly

Be careful though – not all words that end in **ly** are adverbs!

_____   _____
_____   _____
_____   _____
_____   _____
_____   _____

Write down three adverbs that might be used with each of these verbs. One has been written in for you.

2 speak **3** watch

quietly _____ _____   _____ _____ _____

4 throw **5** eat

_____ _____ _____   _____ _____ _____

In each of the empty spaces write the adverb that goes with the description in the top half of the box. One has been done for you.

6 with kindness — kindly

7 in a lazy way —

8 in a way that is not expected —

9 with excitement —

10 with happiness —

11 in an impatient way —

12 Write a few sentences using some of these adverbs.

_____

_____

_____

_____

English crossword

This crossword will test your knowledge of English! The clues are on the opposite page.

➡ ACROSS

2 This punctuation mark makes you pause in a sentence. (5 letters)

4 You probably use this conjunction more than any other. (3 letters)

5 This is the name for a 'doing' word – a word that refers to an action. (4 letters)

7 A group of letters found at the end of a word. (6 letters)

⬇ DOWN

1 This type of word names something. (4 letters)

3 This type of word describes how an action is done. (6 letters)

5 There are five of these in the alphabet. (6 letters)

6 A group of letters found at the beginning of a word. (6 letters)

Story outlines

It can be fun to write the **story plans** of well-known traditional tales. Here is a story frame. Fill in the boxes for the story of Little Red Riding Hood.

Problem	Little Red Riding Hood didn't listen to her mum's advice.
Characters	*Who was in the story?*
Setting	*The places the story is set go here.*
Beginning	
Middle	
End	
Conclusion	*Does Red Riding Hood learn a lesson?*

Answers and Hints

In some instances there may be more than one possible answer so you may need to check that the answer your child has given is reasonable. As long as your child's answer makes sense and has shown they understand the question, you should mark it right. Sometimes the question will ask them to fill in facts about themselves, or to express an opinion, or to create their own piece of work. You may want to judge your child's effort for yourself, but please remember that encouragement is always more helpful than criticism.

PAGE 5
1 apples **2** apricots **3** bananas **4** blackberries **5** cherries **6** figs **7** grapes **8** lemons **9** nectarines **10** oranges **11** peaches **12** plums

PAGE 6

PAGE 7
synonyms pairs (any order): protect–guard, procession–parade, brave–heroic, mail–post, occasionally–sometimes, rare–unusual, seashore–beach, apartment–flat, drizzle–shower

PAGE 8
connected pairs: catch–caught, know–knew, speak–spoke, lead–led, stand–stood, break–broke, go–went, see–saw, keep–kept, think–thought   The past tense verbs here are tricky because they do not end in ed.

PAGE 9
common nouns (any order): ship, courage, flowers, cinema
proper nouns (any order): Apollo, Russia, Suzanne
collective nouns (any order): team, tribe, swarm
Most nouns in English are common nouns.

PAGES 10 & 11
Encourage your child to become familiar with how to use dictionaries and thesauruses, particularly those designed especially for children.   **1** 11   **2** 3   **3** Your child should have written something like 'nibble is to eat a little at a time, devour is to eat quickly and greedily'. If your child has trouble defining these words, discuss the difference between them or refer to the definitions given in a dictionary.   **4** Your child should have changed 'enter' to 'join in', 'put her name down for' or 'take part in'.   **5** excellent (possible answers): brilliant, superb, marvellous, great; exclaimed: shouted, called, cried; expand: grow larger, increase in size, get bigger, swell

PAGES 12 & 13
across: (1) bread, (4) cereal, (6) toast, (7) coffee
down: (1) biscuits, (2) tea, (3) fruit, (5) lettuce

PAGES 14 & 15
1 (adjectives, any order) glorious, sad, disappointing, wonderful, essential, dangerous, round, moist, clean, tough   **2–9** There are lots of possible answers, so provided your child has written three adjectives which could be used to describe each word you should mark them correct.

PAGE 16
correct spellings (in the order in which they appear): brother, sometimes, swimming, birthday, different, paper, balloons, great, children, clothes   Encouraged your child to proof-read their own writing, looking for mistakes caused by carelessness or writing too quickly.

PAGE 17
opposite pairs (any order): distant–near, untidy–neat, true–false, never–always, smooth–uneven, dull–bright, quiet–noisy, hairy–bald, certain–unsure

PAGE 18

2 Check your child has chosen words with double consonants in the middle (possible words: fiddle, middle, muddle, cuddle, simmer, stubble, rubble, huddle, little, stammer).

PAGE 19
Practising using a writing frame reminds your child of the structure a story needs. Talk to your child about how the story has a beginning, a middle and an end, and what happens in each section.

PAGES 20 & 21
1 2   **2** angry, bad-tempered   **3** crowded   **4** between cross and crow   **5** Your child's answers should reflect these definitions: cucumber (noun) a long green vegetable usually eaten raw with cold food; customer (noun) a person who buys something in a shop.

PAGE 22
You will need to check your child has used adjectives and adverbs correctly. If your child is having trouble thinking of interesting words, you may need to discuss with them the kinds of words they could use.

PAGE 23
1 to   **2** two   **3** to   **4** to   **5** too   **6** to   **7** to   **8** to   **9** too   **10** to   **11** two   **12** two   Check your child has used the words correctly in their own sentences.

PAGE 24
1 (any order) wade, write, think, squash, meet, greet, add, break, exclaim, carry   **2** Check your child's sentences show that they have understood the meaning of the words they have chosen and have used them correctly as verbs.

PAGE 25
1 (rhyming pairs, any order) could–would, bone–stone, tough–rough, four–pour, dough–though, none–done, bough–plough   **2** Check your child has chosen words that sound the same for their nonsense rhyme.

PAGE 26
Check you child has correctly spelt the names of the months in the boxes and in the alphabetical list.   **1** April   **2** August   **3** December   **4** February   **5** January   **6** July   **7** June   **8** March   **9** May   **10** November   **11** October   **12** September

PAGE 27
Some of these word chains can be completed in several different ways, but as long as only one letter at a time is changed and the words are proper English words, mark it right. Here is one possible answer for each.   **2** (missing words) fell, felt, pelt   **3** moan, mean, bean   **4** face, fact, fast   **5** post, port, sort   **6** fire, fine, mine   Check that your child's own word chains fit the rules.

PAGE 28
1 there   **2** their   **3** there   **4** they're   **5** their, there   **6** there, their

PAGE 29
1 (circled adverbs) quietly, carefully, quickly, greedily, happily
2 quickly   3 gently   4 loudly   5 carefully

PAGES 30 & 31
Encourage your child to use the contents and index pages of books.   1 chapter 7   2 page 49   3 chapter 2   4 page 81
5 chapters 3 and 6   6 Check your child's questions and answers to see whether they have understood how a contents page works.

PAGES 32 & 33
1 "I'll find you some special fire weed," replied the knight kindly.
2 The little dragon said, "Does it taste nice?"   3 "It's a little peppery," the knight remarked.   4 "I think," said the little dragon, "I might like it."   5 "Don't eat it so quickly," shouted the knight. "You'll get hiccups!"   6 "I don't think that it is going to work," cried the little dragon.   7 "Try clearing your throat," laughed the knight.   8 "Ahhhhhh!" coughed the little dragon. "That's much better!"   9 "Ow!" yelled the knight. "I'm going home before you do any more damage."   Note that in the last two examples, the speaker's second remark is a new sentence, so it begins with a capital letter (and, instead of a comma, a full stop is placed after the speaker's name).

PAGES 34 & 35
1 I wore tight, yellow, flowery leggings.   2 It was the biggest, shiniest, spottiest ball I had ever seen.   3 Grandad had a tiny, cluttered, wooden shed.   4 The kittens made small, mewling, pitiful cries.   5 The Vikings were said to be fierce, bloodthirsty and merciless warriors.   6 My friend was clever, pretty and talented.   8 Mum had bread, tea, bacon, eggs and milk on her shopping list.   9 I saw soap, shampoo, conditioner, bubble bath, toothpaste and toothbrushes on our bathroom shelf.   10 There were Alsatians, Dalmatians, Labradors, poodles and greyhounds at the dog show.   11 Miss Old, Mr Dobbs, Mr Chang, Mrs Wart and my dad are going on the school trip.   12 We had snow, rain, hail and sunshine on Thursday morning.   7 & 13 Writing their own sentences will help your child think about where commas are needed.

PAGE 36
1 (joined up words) washable, hopeful, childlike, heroic, roadworthy   2 (completed words) careful, lifelike, angelic, readable

PAGE 37
rhyming pairs (any order): phone–groan, mane–rain, grow–though, great–crate, worm–squirm, haze–days, group–loop

PAGE 38
message reads: congratulations you've cracked the code!

PAGE 39
1 (correct definition) a wide, natural stream of water   2 a high, steep piece of land close to the sea   3 a large area of water surrounded by land   4 a very high hill   5 the land next to the sea   6 water falling straight down over rocks

PAGE 40
1 It is dark tonight.   2 It is launch day tomorrow.   3 It is an exciting programme.   4 its   5 its   6 It's

PAGE 41
Your child's answers should reflect these meanings; check that they have recognised the significance of the prefixes.
1 (bicycle) a two-wheeled vehicle moved by pushing pedals with your feet; (binoculars) an instrument with lenses for both eyes used for making distant objects seem nearer   2 (tricycle) a three-wheeled cycle; (triangle) a shape with three sides
3 (quadrangle) a square courtyard; (quadruplets) four children born at one birth   4 (pentagon) a shape with five sides; (pentathlon) an athletic contest with five events   5 (centimetre) one hundreth of a metre; (century) one hundred years

PAGES 42 & 43
1 in the Town Hall   2 24 and 25 July   3 Hamilton Park
4 the Mayor of Birkdale   5 Birkdale Station   6 3 p.m., 25 July   7 car, bus or train   8 phone the telephone number given (0157 793 8462)

PAGE 44
3 angle   4 lead   5 astonish   6 after   7 talk   8 hope   9 cycle
10 real   11 usual   12 turn

PAGE 45
Check to see that your child has used sensible adverbs, and talk to them about how they made their choices (what other words could they have used?).

PAGE 46
1 as fast as a cheetah/leopard, as wise as an owl, as cunning as a fox, as sweet as sugar, as green as grass, as white as a sheet
2 The conventional answers would be: leaf, fire, peacock, nails/iron; but if your child has invented their own similes, check that the comparisons are appropriate.   3 Similes that are overused can become clichés, so it is good practice to think of alternative comparisons. By making up their own similes, your child is using language creatively.

PAGE 47
1 fire   2 face   3 film   4 feather   5 fish   6 fan   7 face, fan, feather, film, fire, fish

PAGE 48
2 bank   3 light   4 bill   5 ruler   6 park   7 foot   8 stamp

PAGE 49
2 (missing word) stopped   3 slept   4 slipped   5 keep
6 hurried   7 worry   8 leave   9 fall   10 was

PAGES 50 & 51
You may need to remind your child that nouns are the words we use to name things, verbs are the words we use to describe actions ('doing words') and adjectives are words that describe nouns.   1 (your child should have chosen four words) wood, stone, towers, walls, defences, people, attack, ditches, moats, armies, way, battering rams, arrows, soldiers, oil, attackers, food
2 built, needed, protect, lived, called, climb, force, pour, surround, ran out, surrender   3 but, and, because, or, until   4 earliest, high, thick, strong, deep, enemy, boiling

PAGE 52
1 "Give it to me at once!"   2 "I'm knitting a scarf," she explained.   3 "What's the score?"   4 "How many do you want?"
5 "I'm very sleepy," she replied.   6 "Put that back!"   7 "Why do you want it?"   8 "I enjoy watching videos," he said.   9 "Go away!" she cried.   10 "Where am I?"   It is not essential to have speech marks in the answers to 1, 3, 4, 6, and 10; the assumption is that someone is saying the words, although this may not be obvious to a child of this age.

PAGE 53
1 smaller   2 hungrier   3 smellier   4 darker   5 louder
Check that your child has followed the rules for changing adjectives into comparatives.

PAGES 54 & 55
1 a jet engine   2 it is a proper noun   3 jogger   4 between jigsaw puzzle and job   5 Your child's definitions should reflect the answers given here: January (noun) the first month of the year; juggle (verb) to keep several things in the air by throwing and catching them again; junior (adjective) a younger person, or a less important person.

PAGES 56 & 57
Writing a letter will familiarise your child with the standard layout. It also provides an opportunity to do some creative writing.

PAGES 58 & 59
1 (adverbs) powerfully, hurriedly, gradually, craftily, tenderly, carefully, loudly, energetically, affectionately, cleverly
2–5 There are lots of possible answers, so provided your child has written three adjectives which could be used to describe each word you should mark them correct.   7 lazily   8 unexpectedly
9 excitedly   10 happily   11 impatiently   12 Check that your child has written sentences that use the adverbs sensibly.

PAGES 60 & 61
across: (2) comma, (4) and, (5) verb, (7) suffix
down: (1) noun, (3) adverb, (5) vowels, (6) prefix

PAGE 62
Using a story plan to break down a well-known story into its essential parts is good practice in helping your child plan their own stories.